The Official
2014
FIFA World Cup
Brazil™
FACT FILE

Keir Radnedge

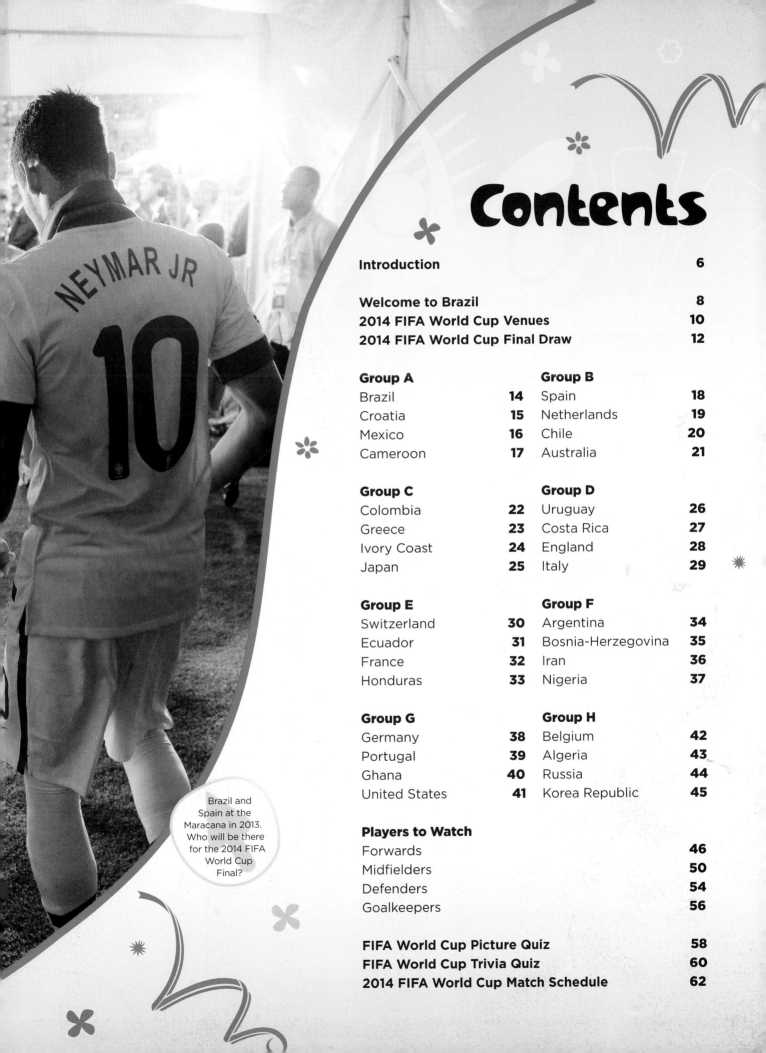

Contents

Brazil and Spain at the Maracana in 2013. Who will be there for the 2014 FIFA World Cup Final?

Introduction

The 2014 FIFA World Cup is an exciting journey into the future combined with massive appreciation of the twists and turns of the event's great history. Brazil is one of the most progressive nations of the 21st century yet it is also a country steeped in football's great traditions and great deeds. No other nation can boast five victories in the FIFA World Cup or such an extensive historical armoury of exciting individuals.

Not that the land of the 'beautiful game' has always been a land of football celebration: there have been tears of pain as well as tears of delight. The most notably dark day in the history of Brazilian football was in 1950 when they lost the final match of the FIFA World Cup against their southern neighbours from Uruguay.

That defeat has haunted not merely Brazilian football but all of Brazil since that day. Now, history is coming full circle. Once more, 64 years on, Brazil is the host nation of the FIFA World Cup and among their 31 rivals from all around the planet will be Uruguay.

Brazil is a vast nation. As FIFA president Sepp Blatter says: "This is not a country but a continent." The game was probably brought to Brazil in the late 19th century by Charles Miller, a student returning home to Sao Paulo from school in England. Simultaneously, another son of immigrants – Oscar Cox – was organising the first games and championship up in Rio de Janeiro.

In 1919 Brazil's new national team won the Copa America for the first time, thanks to the inspiration of their original superstar, Arthur Friedenreich. They failed in the first round of the inaugural FIFA World Cup in Uruguay in 1930 but they are now

The statue of Jesus Christ looks down on Rio de Janeiro and the Maracana stadium.

Modern sculpture in the Three Powers Square, Brasilia, symbolizes togetherness.

the only nation who can lay claim to having been present in all the finals tournaments.

The 20th FIFA World Cup will be staged in 12 venues the length and breadth of Brazil, from the cool south of Porto Alegre to the heat and humidity of Manaus in the Amazon basin. It is a FIFA World Cup which will test the nation's transport and general infrastructure as never before and throws up the footballing fascination of whether a European team can win the FIFA World Cup in the Americas for the first time.

South America has played host on only four previous occasions: Uruguay in 1930, Brazil in 1950, Chile in 1962 and Argentina in 1978. South Americans have won every time: respectively Uruguay (twice), Brazil and Argentina. On two of those four occasions the hosts have triumphed. Brazil even underlined host power by dismissing reigning world and European champions Spain by 3–0 in last year's final of the Confederations Cup, the FIFA World Cup 'rehearsal'.

The qualifying competition for the finals comprised 820 matches between 203 national teams (out of an original entry of 208) with goals scored at the rate of 2.87 per game. The totality of qualifying drama and expectation from the finals prompted a record rush for tickets in the early sales phases.

Brazil is a country featuring an amazing mix of historical, cultural and tourist opportunities. Football fans from all around the world want to share, with Brazilians, a unique event in the history of world sport.

A FIFA World Cup float during the famous Rio Carnival parade. The player is Ronaldo.

Walk along the famous Ipanema Beach in Rio de Janeiro and you will see dozens of football games being played.

Welcome to the Football Country

FIFA WORLD CUP Brasil

Maybe the game's rhythm struck a chord with the carnival atmosphere that seems so prevalent in the country, but, for whatever reason, over the years Brazil has been able to bring its national personality to the game of football – casual, contented, relaxed and playful – like no other nation on earth.

Doubt remains as to who can truly be called Brazil's Father of Football – some sources claim Charles Miller, the English-educated son of a businessman, could claim the title, others suggest it belongs to a Scottish dye-worker called Thomas Donohue – but what cannot be questioned is that from the moment the first ball was kicked in the 1890s, football's popularity spread rapidly throughout the country and soon became interwoven into the very fabric of Brazilian culture.

Not that success on the global stage was instantaneous. Brazil travelled across the border into Uruguary for the inaugural 1930 FIFA World Cup full of optimism, but a 2–1 opening-game defeat to Yugoslavia left their dreams of success in tatters. And things grew no better in Italy, in 1934: Brazil lost 3–1 to Spain in the first round of what was at this time a knockout competition.

But then the Samba Boys slowly began to find their dancing feet. They reached the semi-finals in 1938, finished second, as tournament hosts, in 1950 and then reached the quarter-finals in 1954. Then came 1958: spearheaded by a youthful Pele, Brazil marched to the title playing a brand of football that was admired around the globe.

It served as a blueprint for what would become one of the most dominant spells in international football history. Brazil retained the 1962 FIFA World Cup and won again in 1970; the only blemish came in England in 1966. In contrast, the 1970 team is widely considered the best in football history and the team's performances in Mexico did much to attract a generation of global fans. All of a sudden,

Cafu lifted the FIFA World Cup after Brazil defeated Germany 2–0 in the 2002 Final.

the Brazilian football shirt epitomised flair and footballing perfection.

But the manner and style of Brazil's success at the 1970 FIFA World Cup became a curse for future teams: flair became the byword for Brazilian football and without the players to match their famous forebears (with the exception the 1982 FIFA World Cup) success became difficult to repeat. Glory did not return until the 1994 FIFA World Cup – and then it was achieved with a less glittering style of football. Brazil won again in 2002, and there was a little more artistry than eight years earlier. It remains Brazil's last triumph, but the style of the victories in those golden years evokes vivid pictures of how the beautiful game can be played and ensures that a nation can continue to dream. Football has many homes, but only Brazil can claim to be its spiritual one.

The Brazil team that won the 1970 FIFA World Cup is considered by many experts to be the greatest team ever assembled.

2014 FIFA World Cup Mascot Fuleco greets Brazil football legend Ronaldo in 2012.

MEET THE MASCOT

Unveiled in September 2012, the official mascot for the 2014 FIFA World Cup is a three-banded armadillo, an endangered species in Brazil. His name is Fuleco – a fusion of the words *futebol* (football) and *ecologia* (ecology) – and he wears the colours of the Brazilian national flag. He attracted more than 1.7 million (48 percent) of all votes cast between September and November 2012. Fuleco has since spent his time touring Brazil (89 percent of the country's population have said they have seen him). FIFA's Marketing Director, Thierry Weil, said of Fuleco, "Not only is he well-known and recognised by the vast majority of Brazilians, he also seems to have built up a rapport with football fans and is a popular figure."

The Venues

On 31 May 2009, 12 host cities covering the length and breadth of Brazil were chosen to host games at the 2014 FIFA World Cup. Six of those cities will host matches at brand-new stadiums, five existing stadiums have been refurbished, while the stadium in Brasilia has been demolished and rebuilt.

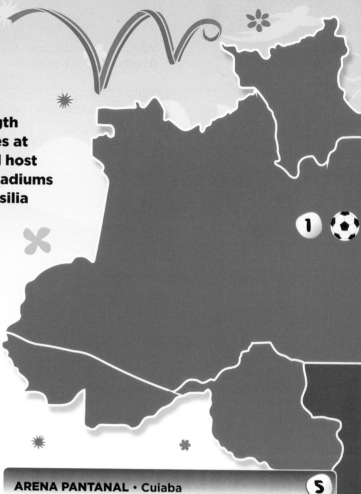

ARENA AMAZONIA · Manaus ①

Situated in Manaus in the heart of the Amazon rainforest, the area may not be a traditional hotbed of Brazilian football but the magnificent Arena Amazonia is sure to set fans' pulses racing. The refurbished 42,374-capacity stadium, designed to resemble a straw basket for which the region is famous, will play host to four group matches at the 2014 FIFA World Cup.

ESTADIO NACIONAL · Brasilia ②

The capital city's Estadio Mane Garrincha has been all but demolished to make way for the latest addition to Brasilia's eye-catching, modern skyline: the architecturally imposing, environmentally-friendly, metal-roofed, 68,009-capacity Estadio Nacional. Completed in 2012, the stadium – the second largest of the tournament's 12 venues – will host seven games at the 2014 FIFA World Cup, one of them a quarter-final tie.

ARENA DA BAIXADA · Curitaba ③

The Arena da Baixada underwent an extensive reconstruction in the late 1990s and has long been considered as one of Brazil's most modern and best-appointed venues. It came as little surprise, therefore, when the 41,456-capacity stadium was selected as one of the 12 venues for the 2014 FIFA World Cup, during which it will play host to four first-round group matches.

ESTADIO BEIRA-RIO · Porto Alegre ④

The largest football ground in the southern part of the country and the home of Brazilian giants Internacional, the Estadio Beira-Rio – nicknamed the "Giant of Beira-Rio" – enjoys a spectacular location on reclaimed land on the banks of the River Guaiba. Refurbished for the 2014 FIFA World Cup, the 48.849-capacity stadium will host five matches during the tournament, including one round-of-16 tie.

ARENA PANTANAL · Cuiaba ⑤

Specially constructed for the 2014 FIFA World Cup, during which it will play host to four group matches, the 42,968-capacity Arena Pantanal has been based on sustainability, in keeping with the flora-and-fauna rich region to which it belongs – all the wood used in the construction came from certified sources. Two local clubs, Mixto and Operario, will make the stadium their home after the tournament is over.

ESTADIO DAS DUNAS · Natal ⑥

Designed to resemble the undulating sand dunes for which the Natal region in famous, the brand-new, innovative, 42,086-capacity Estadio das Dunas (completed in 2013) stands on the site of the former Estadio Joao Claudio de Vasconcelos (otherwise known as the Machadao). The stadium will play host to four group matches during the 2014 FIFA World Cup.

ESTADIO MINEIRAO · Belo Horizonte ⑦

The 62,547-capacity Estadio Mineirao, the home of Atletico Mineiro and Cruzeiro and one of the most historic stadiums in Brazilian football, has undergone a complete overhaul in readiness for the 2014 FIFA World Cup – including adding facilities to capture and store up to 6.27 million litres of reusable rainwater. Originally constructed in 1965, it is universally known as the Mineirao.

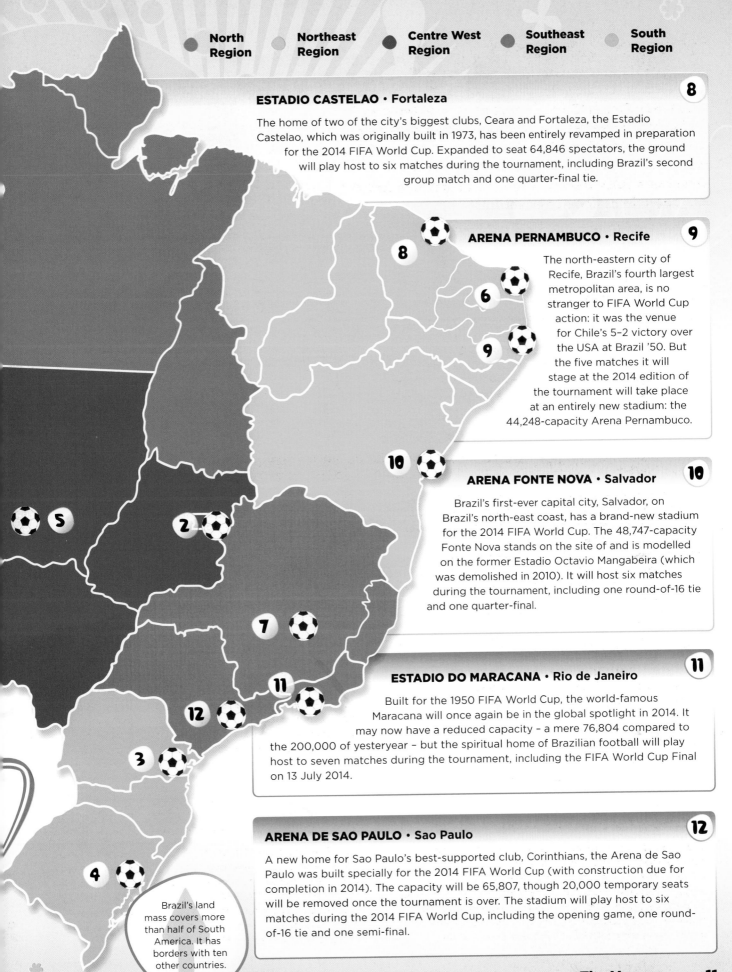

North Region   Northeast Region   Centre West Region   Southeast Region   South Region

ESTADIO CASTELAO · Fortaleza — 8

The home of two of the city's biggest clubs, Ceara and Fortaleza, the Estadio Castelao, which was originally built in 1973, has been entirely revamped in preparation for the 2014 FIFA World Cup. Expanded to seat 64,846 spectators, the ground will play host to six matches during the tournament, including Brazil's second group match and one quarter-final tie.

ARENA PERNAMBUCO · Recife — 9

The north-eastern city of Recife, Brazil's fourth largest metropolitan area, is no stranger to FIFA World Cup action: it was the venue for Chile's 5–2 victory over the USA at Brazil '50. But the five matches it will stage at the 2014 edition of the tournament will take place at an entirely new stadium: the 44,248-capacity Arena Pernambuco.

ARENA FONTE NOVA · Salvador — 10

Brazil's first-ever capital city, Salvador, on Brazil's north-east coast, has a brand-new stadium for the 2014 FIFA World Cup. The 48,747-capacity Fonte Nova stands on the site of and is modelled on the former Estadio Octavio Mangabeira (which was demolished in 2010). It will host six matches during the tournament, including one round-of-16 tie and one quarter-final.

ESTADIO DO MARACANA · Rio de Janeiro — 11

Built for the 1950 FIFA World Cup, the world-famous Maracana will once again be in the global spotlight in 2014. It may now have a reduced capacity – a mere 76,804 compared to the 200,000 of yesteryear – but the spiritual home of Brazilian football will play host to seven matches during the tournament, including the FIFA World Cup Final on 13 July 2014.

ARENA DE SAO PAULO · Sao Paulo — 12

A new home for Sao Paulo's best-supported club, Corinthians, the Arena de Sao Paulo was built specially for the 2014 FIFA World Cup (with construction due for completion in 2014). The capacity will be 65,807, though 20,000 temporary seats will be removed once the tournament is over. The stadium will play host to six matches during the 2014 FIFA World Cup, including the opening game, one round-of-16 tie and one semi-final.

Brazil's land mass covers more than half of South America. It has borders with ten other countries.

The Venues   11

2014 FIFA World Cup Brazil™ Final Draw

The Final Draw for the 2014 FIFA World Cup which began in sombre style, featuring a tribute to Nelson Mandela and an appeal for unity from FIFA president Sepp Blatter, ended with a swirl of expectation ahead of the finals in Brazil.

The hosts and favourites were drawn to kick off against Croatia; England (by the hands of Sir Geoff Hurst) were handed a hot and humid start against Italy in Manaus; Germany's Joachim Low was charted to come up against the man who launched his national team career in now-US coach Jurgen Klinsmann; and champions Spain were despatched to begin against the Dutchmen they beat in the 2010 final. Worldwide television viewers and an audience of directors, officials and media attended the draw in the coastal resort of Costa do Sauipe, some 50 miles beyond the northern venue city of Salvador.

The death of Mandela, iconic former President of South Africa, was acknowledged in an opening montage of his involvement in bringing the FIFA World Cup to South Africa four years ago plus a brief silent tribute. Then it was on with the show, led by presidents Dilma Rousseff of Brazil and Blatter of FIFA.

Blatter took the opportunity to appeal to Brazilians to forget about repeating the Confederations Cup demonstrations while the

FIFA World Cup party was in full swing. He said: "It was time that the World Cup came back to Brazil. Next year it will 60 years since Brazil first organised the World Cup . . . so please come together and join everybody involved because it's a game for you and also for fans around the world in the 208 other national associations. It will be a great World Cup, perhaps the greatest of all times."

That was the cue for Vicente Del Bosque, manager of Spain's 2010 FIFA World Cup winners, to bring the trophy itself on stage followed by a parade of Brazilian favourites including Ronaldo, Marta, Bebeto and, of course, Pele.

Finally, 48 minutes into the show, the all-important goldfish bowls appeared on stage plus the 'fishermen' in Mario Kempes, Fabio Cannavaro, Lothar Matthaus, Zinedine Zidane, Hierro, Cafu, Alcides Ghiggia and Sir Geoff Hurst.

Overseeing the occasion was Jerome Valcke, FIFA's French secretary-general with the television slice of proceedings being run by the husband-and-wife team of Rodrigo Hilbert and Fernanda Lima.

As arranged in advance, Brazil were slotted into Group A. The luck of the draw then placed Spain in Group B, Colombia in Group C, Uruguay in Group D, Switzerland in Group E, Argentina in Group F, Germany in Group G and Belgium in the travel-friendly Group H.

Italy, denied a top seeding by the decision to use October's FIFA/Coca-Cola World Ranking rather than the November listing, were then drawn into the feared 'floater' slot, in Group D. The rest of the draw was then duly rolled out.

Group G (Germany, Portugal, Ghana and United States) appeared the likely 'Group of Death' followed by Group D (Uruguay, Costa Rica, England, Italy). The make-up of the latter meant that at least one former FIFA World Cup-winning nation will not make it through to the knockout stage.

Of course, given the quality of the line-up, there could be more famous fallers at the first fence.

Presidents Dilma Rousseff of Brazil and Sepp Blatter of FIFA welcome the world.

Brazilian icon Pele takes centre stage in Costa do Sauipe.

The draw in full swing under the command of Jerome Valcke.

Group A	Group B
Brazil	Spain
Croatia	Netherlands
Mexico	Chile
Cameroon	Australia
Group C	**Group D**
Colombia	Uruguay
Greece	Costa Rica
Ivory Coast	England
Japan	Italy
Group E	**Group F**
Switzerland	Argentina
Ecuador	Bosnia-Herzegovina
France	Iran
Honduras	Nigeria
Group G	**Group H**
Germany	Belgium
Portugal	Algeria
Ghana	Russia
United States	Korea Republic

Brazil
Record six in sight

Group A

Brazil are the world's favourite 'other' football nation because of an endless flow of entertainingly talented players. The 'Beautiful Game' began with legendary Leonidas in the 1930s, Ademir and Zizinho in the 1940s, the matchless generation of Pele and Garrincha between 1958 and 1970 then the likes of Romario and Ronaldo. Luiz Felipe Scolari was recalled as manager in November 2012 to try to repeat his FIFA World Cup-winning magic from 2002. Crucial in attack for him is Barcelona forward Neymar.

FACT FILE

Founded: 1914

National stadium: Maracana, Rio de Janeiro/ Estadio Nacional, Brasilia

Nickname: Canarinha/ Seleção

Route to the finals: Qualified automatically as hosts

FIFA World Ranking: 10

FIFA World Cup Finals appearances: 19

Winners: 1958, 1962, 1970, 1994, 2002

Ones to watch: Neymar, Thiago Silva, Paulinho

Coach: Luiz Felipe Scolari

Outstanding defender Thiago Silva will be Brazil's captain in 2014.

Brazil will have one of the potent attacks at the 2014 FIFA World Cup, with talents such as Fred sure to shine.

Splat Stat
Brazil have won the FIFA World Cup on a record five occasions and, since its creation in 1930, are the only national team to have competed in all 19 finals tournaments.

Any players wearing the famous colours of Brazil must be respected.

Croatia
Youth and experience

Group A

Croatia, at 22, may be one of the youngest footballing nations at the 2014 FIFA World Cup finals but they are one of the most respected. They finished third on their finals debut in 1998, qualified in 2002 and 2006, but missed out in 2010. Captain Darijo Srna is Croaitia's record appearance-maker and he links the old and new generations, while Luka Modric pulls the midfield strings. Croatia finished second in their group then beat Iceland in the play-offs. The only negative was a red card for match-winner Mario Mandzukic, who is thus suspended for the opening game against hosts Brazil.

FACT FILE

Founded: 1992 (previously 1912–19 and 1941–44)

National stadium: Maksimir, Zagreb

Nickname: Vatreni (Fiery ones)

Route to the finals: Runners-up in UEFA Group A, then 0–0, 2–0 (2–0 agg) v Iceland

FIFA World Ranking: 16

FIFA World Cup Finals appearances: 3

Winners: None

Ones to watch: Mario Mandzukic, Darijo Srna, Luka Modric

Coach: Niko Kovac

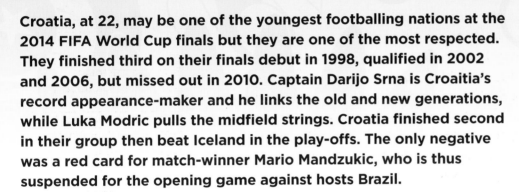

Luka Modric has established himself as one of Europe's most creative playmakers.

Mario Mandzukic was Croatia's four-goal top scorer in the qualifiers, but he will miss the opening game.

Splat Stat
Davor Suker has improved his status as Croatia's all-time top scorer with 45 goals (including top-scoring six at the 1998 FIFA World Cup) by becoming FA president.

Croatia were third on their FIFA World Cup finals debut in 1998. Their aim is two places higher in 2014.

Mexico
A golden generation

Group A

In the early years of the FIFA World Cup, Mexico qualified regularly but were easy victims for almost everyone. When El Tri hosted the FIFA World Cup for the second time in 1986 they had found their international feet. Mexico's clubs are among the richest and most powerful in the Americas and the under-23s outplayed Brazil to win the gold medal at the London 2012 Olympic Games. However, they made very hard work of qualifying and advanced only after winning an intercontinental play-off against New Zealand. And no attack with 'Chicharito' Hernandez and Oribe Peralta can be underrated.

FACT FILE

Founded: 1927

National stadium: Azteca, Mexico City

Nickname: El Tri

Route to the finals: Winners of CONCACAF third round Group B, fourth in fourth round group then 5–1, 4–2 (9–3 agg) v New Zealand in the intercontinental play-offs

FIFA World Ranking: 21

FIFA World Cup Finals appearances: 14

Winners: None

Ones to watch: Javier Hernandez, Oribe Peralta, Giovani dos Santos

Coach: Miguel Herrera

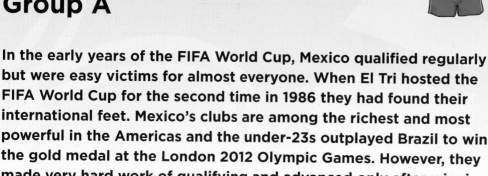

Oribe Peralta proved his match-winning qualities against New Zealand in the play-off.

Splat Stat
Mexico had four coaches in the qualifying competition. Jose Manuel De la Torre, Luis Fernando Tena and Victor Vucetich were all sacked before Miguel Herrera finished what they started.

Javier "Chicharito" Hernandez has honed his attacking talents in the Premier League.

Mexico beat New Zealand 9–3 on aggregate in the decisive play-off round.

Cameroon
Roaring for more

Group A

Cameroon have been one of the most popular African contenders ever since the 1990 FIFA World Cup finals. Then Roger Milla's team started by defeating champions Argentina and succumbed only to England in extra time in the quarter-finals. German coach Volker Finke's team dropped five points in their qualifying group and managed only five open-play goals in six games. They had improved when they met Tunisia in their play-off. The Indomitable Lions drew 0–0 away and won 4–1 in Yaounde, thanks to two goals from Jean Makoun, the central midfielder from French club Rennes.

FACT FILE

Founded: 1959
National stadium: Ahmadou Ahidjo, Yaounde
Nickname: Indomitable Lions
Route to the finals: Winners of CAF second round Group I then 0–0, 4–1 (4–1 agg) v Tunisia
FIFA World Ranking: 50
FIFA World Cup Finals appearances: 6
Winners: None
Ones to watch: Samuel Eto'o, Jean Makoun, Alexandre Song
Coach: Volker Finke

Samuel Eto'o is the Indomitable Lions' top scorer with 55 goals in more than 100 games.

Splat Stat
Cameroon had extra help in their qualifying effort. Togo beat them 2–0 in Lome but the Indomitable Lions were awarded a 3–0 win because Togo had fielded an ineligible player, Alaixys Romao.

Alexandre Song switched to Cameroon after playing youth football for France.

Cameroon are now virtual ever-presents in the FIFA World Cup finals from Africa.

Spain
Champions' challenge

Group B

Spain have commanded world football for the past six years, ever since their Euro 2008 triumph sent them on a slalom of three successive top titles. These included a long-overdue FIFA World Cup triumph in South Africa in 2010. Simultaneously they have long been established atop the FIFA World Rankings. However, defeat for the world and European champions by Brazil in the 2013 Confederations Cup Final hinted Spain may be vulnerable when a team built around now-ageing players return to South America.

FACT FILE

Founded: 1909
National stadium: Estadio Santiago Bernabeu, Madrid
Nickname: La Roja
Route to the finals: Winners UEFA Group I
FIFA World Ranking: 1
FIFA World Cup Finals appearances: 13
Winners: 2010
Ones to watch: Sergio Ramos, Andres Iniesta, Xavi Hernandez
Coach: Vicente Del Bosque

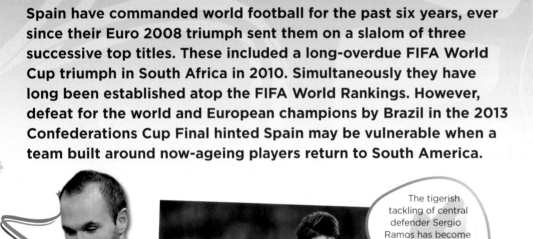

The tigerish tackling of central defender Sergio Ramos has become a key element in Spain's recent success.

Splat Stat
Spain set a world record of 29 competitive matches unbeaten over three years from the second match of the 2010 FIFA World Cup to the semi-final of the 2013 FIFA Confederations Cup Brazil.

Andres Iniesta scored the winning goal late in the 2010 FIFA World Cup Final.

Twice European champions and 2010 FIFA World Cup winners, can anyone stop Spain?

Netherlands
Repairing the image

Group B

The era of Johan Cruyff's total football is long gone and so are the Euro-dominating days of Ruud Gullit and Marco Van Basten. The Dutch have finished FIFA World Cup runners-up three times and owe it to their fans to erase memories of the ugly second-place finish behind Spain in South Africa in 2010. Robin Van Persie was the European qualifiers' main man with 11 goals. Only Germany scored more than the Dutchmen's 34. They won nine of their 10 games and dropped points only in a 2–2 draw with Estonia.

FACT FILE

Founded: 1889
National stadium: Amsterdam ArenA
Nickname: Oranje
Route to the finals: Winners of UEFA Group D
FIFA World Ranking: 9
FIFA World Cup Finals appearances: 9
Winners: None
Ones to watch: Robin Van Persie, Arjen Robben, Rafael Van der Vaart
Coach: Louis Van Gaal

Rafael Van der Vaart has been a key midfielder for the Dutch since 2003.

Splat Stat
Star striker Robin Van Persie hit a hat-trick in an 8–1 thrashing of Hungary. He thus overtook Patrick Kluivert as Holland's all-time top scorer with 41 goals in 81 games.

Arjen Robben aims to make amends for missed chances in the 2010 FIFA World Cup Final.

Runners-up in 2010, the Netherlands want to go one better at the 2014 FIFA World Cup Brazil.

Chile
Change for the better

Group B

Chile surprised themselves as hosts in 1962 by finishing third and have never come as close to the elite again. However, they have continued to produce star individuals such as Carlos Caszely then Ivan Zamorano and now the likes of Barcelona forward Alexis Sanchez. Chile qualified despite changing coach halfway through the campaign when three defeats in a row led to Jorge Sampaoli replacing sacked Claudio Borghi. They were second-top scorers in their group with 29 goals (Argentina scored 35).

FACT FILE

Founded: 1895
National stadium: Estadio Nacional, Santiago
Nickname: La Roja
Route to the finals: Third in CONMEBOL group
FIFA World Ranking: 15
FIFA World Cup Finals appearances: 7
Winners: None
Ones to watch: Alexis Sanchez, Arturo Vidal, Jean Beausejour
Coach: Jorge Sampaoli

Splat Stat
A dramatic late six-game dash of five wins and a draw saw the Chileans qualify for a second FIFA World Cup finals tournament in a row for the first time in their history.

Chile's electric pace on the break depends heavily on Jean Beausejour.

Chile have hit form at the right time for a serious challenge at the 2014 FIFA World Cup Brazil.

Alexis Sanchez showed his talent with two goals against England last November.

Australia
Socceroos on the move

Group B

Australia have proved more of a force each time they have competed in the FIFA World Cup. They did not enter until the 1966 FIFA World Cup and reached the finals for the first time in 1974 in West Germany. It was 32 years before they qualified again but they reached the second round in 2006 and missed out on progress only on goal difference in 2010. German coach Holger Osieck guided them to Brazil but, after two bad defeats in friendlies by Brazil and France, was replaced as manager by Ange Postecoglou.

FACT FILE

Founded: 1961
National stadium: Stadium Australia, Sydney
Nickname: Socceroos
Route to the finals: Winners of AFC third round Group D then runners-up in AFC fourth round Group B
FIFA World Ranking: 58
FIFA World Cup Finals appearances: 3
Winners: None
Ones to watch: Tim Cahill, Lucas Neill, Brett Holman
Coach: Ange Postecoglou

Lucas Neill honed his know-how in 15 years in England.

Splat Stat
Tim Cahill is Australia's all-time leading scorer at the FIFA World Cup finals with three goals out of his country's eight in 10 games, comprising two goals in 2006 and one in 2010.

Tim Cahill was the first Australian to score in the FIFA World Cup finals.

The Socceroos are making their third consecutive FIFA World Cup finals appearance in 2014.

Colombia
Back on track

Group C

Colombia have a chequered FIFA World Cup history. They qualified first in 1962, gave up their hosting opportunity in 1986 and were hit by tragedy in 1994 when defender Andres Escobar was shot dead back home after putting through his own goal in the finals in the United States. A team starring bouffant-haired playmaker Carlos Valderrama and erratic winger Faustino Asprilla lost in the group stages in 1998. Superstar striker Radamel Falcao is leading them back to their first finals since then.

FACT FILE

Founded: 1924
National stadium: Estadio Metropolitano Roberto Melendez, Barranquilla
Nickname: Los Cafeteros
Route to the finals: Runners-up in CONMEBOL group
FIFA World Ranking: 4
FIFA World Cup Finals appearances: 4
Winners: None
Ones to watch: Mario Yepes, Radamel Falcao, James Rodriguez
Coach: Jose Pekerman

Radamel Falcao scored 100-plus goals in his first three seasons in Europe.

Splat Stat
Radamel Falcao set a 17-goal European competition record for Europa League winners Porto in 2010–11. He was then Colombia's nine-goal top scorer on the road to Brazil.

Colombia will be no one's idea of an easy game after strolling through the South Amiercan qualifiers.

"Super" Mario Yepes has commanded Colombia's defence as captain since 2008.

Greece
Something to cheer

Group C

Greece, shock 2004 UEFA European Championship winners, have appeared at the FIFA World Cup only twice before and hope that Brazil might be third time lucky as they try to advance beyond the group stage for the first time. As coach Fernando Santos has noted, that would provide some cheer for the nation after all its economic problems. The spirit and resilience of the squad was illustrated by the play-off defeat of a tough Romanian side. Olympiacos' German-taught striker Konstantidis Mitroglou was the hero with two goals in Athens and one in Bucharest.

FACT FILE

Founded: 1926
National stadium: Olympic Stadium, Athens
Nickname: Pirates
Route to the finals: Runners-up in UEFA Group G then 3–1, 1–1 (4–2 agg) v Romania
FIFA World Ranking: 12
FIFA World Cup Finals appearances: 2
Winners: None
Ones to watch: Georgios Samaras, Dimitrius Salpingidis, Georgios Karagounis
Coach: Fernando Santos

Captain Georgios Karagounis is Greece's record international with more than 130 caps.

Splat Stat
Goalkeeper Orestis Karnezis was the only man to play in every minute of Greece's qualifiying campaign. It amounted to 900 minutes in the group stage and 180 minutes in the play-offs.

Striker Konstantidis Mitroglou played a decisive role for Greece in the play-offs.

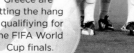

Greece are getting the hang of qualifiying for the FIFA World Cup finals.

Ivory Coast
Last chance saloon

Group C

The Ivorians are in the FIFA World Cup finals for a third consecutive tournament, but this is a last glory opportunity for an ageing nucleus of players, led by ever-dangerous Didier Drogba. He has scored a record 60-plus goals for the Ivory Coast, including at each of the last two FIFA World Cup finals, while Didier Zokora and Manchester City's Yaya Toure provide powerful support from midfield. But the country has only one title to its name, the 1992 African Nations Cup. In 2014, the Elephants' target is to progress to at least the second round.

FACT FILE

Founded: 1960
National stadium: Felix Houphouet-Boigny, Abidjan
Nickname: Elephants
Route to the finals: Winners of CAF second round Group C then 3-1, 1-1 (4-2 agg) v Senegal
FIFA World Ranking: 17
FIFA World Cup Finals appearances: 2
Winners: None
Ones to watch: Didier Drogba, Salomon Kalou, Yaya Toure
Coach: Sabri Lamouchi

Yaya Toure was named as the 2013 African Footballer of the Year, becoming a three-time winner.

Splat Stat
Ivory Coast was undefeated in the qualifying campaign. The Elephants won four times and drew twice with Morocco to top Group C, then beat and drew with Senegal in the play-offs.

Ivory Coast are determined to reach the knockout stage for the first time.

Didier Drogba knows all about success on football's greatest stages.

Japan
Asian champions' challenge

Group C

Japan have made spectacular progress in the international game since the launch of a national professional league in the mid-1990s. At first the national team were about teamwork to the almost total exclusion of individual flair. The evolution of the J.League, however, has helped generate a team mixing disciplined possession football with star quality. As Asian champions the Blue Samurai competed in last year's Confederations Cup in Brazil but crashed out after losing all three group games.

FACT FILE

Founded: 1921
National stadium: International Stadium, Yokohama
Nickname: Blue Samurai
Route to the finals: Runners-up in AFC third round Group C; winners of AFC fourth round Group B
FIFA World Ranking: 47
FIFA World Cup Finals appearances: 4
Winners: None
Ones to watch: Eiji Kawashima, Shinji Kagawa, Keisuke Honda
Coach: Alberto Zaccheroni

Shinji Kagawa's talents were rewarded with Asia's top player prize in 2012.

Splat Stat
Shinji Kagawa became Japan's most costly player when Manchester United paid Borussia Dortmund £17m in 2012. He won German and English league titles in successive seasons.

Keisuke Honda is a danger to any goalkeeper from free kicks.

Japan scored 30 goals and conceded eight in qualifying for the 2014 FIFA World Cup.

Uruguay
The history men

Group D

Ondino Viera, who coached Uruguay at the 1966 finals, said: "Other countries have their history, we have our football." So, even though the Celeste (Sky Blues) needed a play-off victory over Jordan to head north into Brazil, they are always worth their place. Forwards Luis Suarez and Edison Cavani are two of the world's finest strikers, with talent further honed since Uruguay's third-place finish in the South Africa FIFA World Cup 2010. 'Profesor' Oscar Washington Tabarez, at 67, is expected to be the oldest manager at the finals.

FACT FILE

Founded: 1900
National stadium: Centenario, Montevideo
Nickname: Celeste
Route to the finals: Fifth in CONMEBOL group then 5-0, 0-0 (5-0 agg) v Jordan
FIFA World Ranking: 6
FIFA World Cup Finals appearances: 11
Winners: 1930, 1950
Ones to watch: Luis Suarez, Edison Cavani, Diego Godin
Coach: Oscar Washington Tabarez

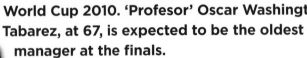

Luis Suarez made his name with Uruguay at the FIFA U-20 World Cup in 2007.

Splat Stat
Uruguay, with a population of 3.2 million, is the smallest country ever to have won the FIFA World Cup (they did so in both 1930 and 1950) and also to have hosted the finals (in 1930).

Uruguay reached the semi-finals of the 2013 FIFA Confederations Cup in Brazil.

Edinson Cavani has ripped apart club defences in Italy and France.

Costa Rica
Winning in translation

Group D

The term "Ticos" – nickname of people from the central American nation – has no direct translation. Perhaps that air of mystery is why they have continually surprised grander football nations and rank No.3 in CONCACAF history behind the much larger nations of United States and Mexico. Colombian coach Jorge Luis Pinto took over for a second time in 2011 to guide them to a surprise second place in the qualifying *liguilla*. Show-stopper was Fulham forward Bryan Ruiz, ably supported by Celso Borges and veteran Alvaro Saborio.

FACT FILE

Founded: 1921
National stadium: Estadio Nacional, San Jose
Nickname: Los Ticos
Route to the finals: Runners-up CONCACAF third round Group B; second in fourth round
FIFA World Ranking: 31
FIFA World Cup Finals appearances: 3
Winners: None
Ones to watch: Bryan Ruiz, Christian Bolanos, Alvaro Saborio
Coach: Jorge Luis Pinto

Goalkeeper Keylor Navas first starred for Costa Rica at the 2003 FIFA World Under-17s in Finland.

Splat Stat
Costa Rica's first FIFA World Cup finals, in 1990, was their best. Under "magician" Bora Milutinovic they lost in round two after progressing from a group featuring Brazil, Scotland and Sweden.

Captain Bryan Ruiz scored in Costa Rica's 2–1 qualifying win against Mexico.

Costa Rica were runners-up to the United States in CONCACAF qualifying.

England
Hodgson's history men

Group D

England enter every FIFA World Cup shouldering the weight of expectation linked back to the 150-year history of the FA and the 1966 FIFA World Cup win. Manager Roy Hodgson had a tough baptism at short notice in the 2012 European Championships and has begun to develop his own team, mixing the 'old guard' such as captain Steven Gerrard, Ashley Cole and star striker Wayne Rooney with new boys such as Jack Wilshere, Danny Welbeck and Daniel Sturridge. They go to Brazil with growing confidence after topping their qualifying group.

FACT FILE

Founded: 1863
National stadium: Wembley, London
Nickname: Three Lions
Route to the finals: Winners of UEFA Group H
FIFA World Ranking: 13
FIFA World Cup Finals appearances: 13
Winners: 1966
Ones to watch: Wayne Rooney, Steven Gerrard, Jack Wilshere
Coach: Roy Hodgson

Wayne Rooney was England's leading scorer in qualifying with seven goals.

Ashley Cole has won every prize at club level with Chelsea.

Splat Stat

England have gone 14 competitive games unbeaten since Roy Hodgson took over from Fabio Capello two years ago. They were knocked out of Euro 2012 by Italy only on penalties.

Expectations may be low but in the eyes of many fans it is always "England expects".

Italy
Europe's most successful

Group D

Italy are Europe's greatest FIFA World Cup competitors. The Azzurri were the continent's first winners, then first triple winners and boast four titles. Their great players have not always played great football but they always play to win. Coach Cesare Prandelli guided them to runners-up spot at Euro 2012 and the nucleus of that team will go to Brazil after an unbeaten qualifying competition. Mario Balotelli, back with Milan after a tempestuous spell at Manchester City, was five-goal top scorer.

Midfielder Daniele Di Rossi is a survivor from Italy's 2006 FIFA World Cup-winning squad.

Pablo Osvaldo was born in Argentina but Italy quickly capitalised on his family background.

Splat Stat
The Azzurri lived up to their mean reputation, in both attack and defence, on the road to Brazil. In their 10 games they scored just 19 goals at the rate of 1.9 per game and conceded nine.

It would be foolish to expect Italy not to have a real chance of a fifth FIFA World Cup.

Switzerland
Banking on teamwork

Group E

Switzerland once went 28 years without reaching the FIFA World Cup finals. After losing in the first round in England in 1966 it was an Englishman, Roy Hodgson, who finally took them back to the finals in 1994. This is their third successive appearance and in Ottmar Hitzfeld they boast one of world football's most respected coaches. The Swiss were undefeated in Group E, winning seven and drawing three games to end seven points clear of runners-up Iceland. Remarkably, their 17 goals were shared among 10 players.

FACT FILE

Founded: 1895
National stadium: Stade de Suisse, Bern
Nickname: La Nati
Route to the finals: Winners UEFA Group E
FIFA World Ranking: 8
FIFA World Cup Finals appearances: 9
Winners: None
Ones to watch: Gokhan Inler, Tranquillo Barnetta, Xherdan Shaqiri
Coach: Ottmar Hitzfeld

Midfielder Gokhan Inler has had a stellar career since his rejection by Fenerbahce in Turkey.

Splat Stat
The Swiss have reached the quarter-finals of the FIFA World Cup on three occasions but a long time ago – in 1934 in Italy, in 1938 in France and then again as the host nation in 1954.

Kosovo-born Xherdan Shaqiri's starring role for Switzerland helped earn him a move to Bayern Munich.

If the Swiss defence continues to be miserly, the forwards must get the goals for them to advance.

Ecuador
Reason to believe

Group E

Ecuador were not certain of qualifying for the finals until the last round of matches when a 2–1 defeat by Chile still provided enough security to see them through on goal difference ahead of Uruguay. Players and staff dedicated their qualifying success to team-rnate Christian Benitez who had died of heart failure, aged 27, weeks earlier while playing for his Qatari club, Al-Jaish. Benitez had scored four goals in the qualifying series. Felipe Caicedo, with seven goals (four penalties) was the main man.

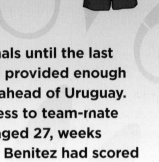

FACT FILE

Founded: 1926
National stadium: Estadio Olimpico Atahualpa, Quito
Nickname: La Tri
Route to the finals: Fourth in CONMEBOL group
FIFA World Ranking: 23
FIFA World Cup Finals appearances: 2
Winners: None
Ones to watch: Antonio Valencia, Edison Mendez, Felipe Caicedo
Coach: Reinaldo Rueda

Splat Stat
Ecuador needed 72 years to reach the FIFA World Cup finals for the first time in 2002 but now make their third appearance in the last four finals tournaments. Their best finish was the second round in 2006.

Veteran midfielder Edison Mendez has more than 100 appearances for Ecuador to his name.

Versatile Antonio Valencia can play anywhere on the right side of defence or attack.

After surprising South America with automatic qualification, can Ecuador create shockwaves in Brazil.

France
Bright blue again

Group E

France have taken almost four years to recover from the 2010 FIFA World Cup South Africa debacle, when the team imploded. It was a shock for fans, with the 1998 FIFA World Cup win and 2006 FIFA World Cup runners-up slot fresh in their memory. Didier Deschamps, who captained France to their 1998 FIFA World Cup and 2000 UEFA European Championship double, has instilled order and discipline on and off the pitch. In the play-offs against Ukraine, France became the first nation ever to overcome a 2–0 first-leg deficit and reach the FIFA World Cup finals.

FACT FILE

Founded: 1890, reorganised 1919

National stadium: Stade de France, Paris/St-Denis

Nickname: Les Bleus

Route to the finals: Runners-up in UEFA Group I then 0-2, 3-0 v Ukraine

FIFA World Ranking: 20

FIFA World Cup Finals appearances: 13

Winners: 1998

Ones to watch: Franck Ribery, Karim Benzema, Hugo Lloris

Coach: Didier Deschamps

Franck Ribery proved a qualifying winner with France and a club winner with Bayern Munich.

Splat Stat
France are Europe's only winners of the three main international trophies: the FIFA World Cup (1998), FIFA Confederations Cup (2001 and 2003) and Olympic Games (1984).

Karim Benzema was voted French Footballer of the Year in 2011 and 2012.

France aim to atone for their poor showing in the 2010 FIFA World Cup in South Africa.

Honduras
Suarez's focus group

Group E

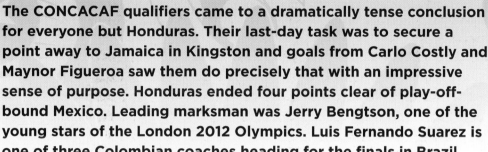

The CONCACAF qualifiers came to a dramatically tense conclusion for everyone but Honduras. Their last-day task was to secure a point away to Jamaica in Kingston and goals from Carlo Costly and Maynor Figueroa saw them do precisely that with an impressive sense of purpose. Honduras ended four points clear of play-off-bound Mexico. Leading marksman was Jerry Bengtson, one of the young stars of the London 2012 Olympics. Luis Fernando Suarez is one of three Colombian coaches heading for the finals in Brazil.

FACT FILE

Founded: 1951
National stadium: Estadio Olimpico Metropolitano, San Pedro Sula
Nickname: Los Catrachos
Route to the finals: Winners of CONCACAF third round, Group C; third in fourth round
FIFA World Ranking: 42
FIFA World Cup Finals appearances: 2
Winners: None
Ones to watch: Maynor Figueroa, Emilio Izaguirre, Jerry Bengtson
Coach: Luis Fernando Suarez

Maynor Figueroa's game has benefited from six years in English football with Wigan Athletic and Hull City.

Splat Stat
Honduras have come a long way since, in 1921, losing their first ever game 10–1 to Guatemala. Some 80 years later they ended third as guests in a top-class Copa America tournament.

Jerry Bengtson hit a FIFA World Cup qualifying hat-trick against Canada.

Given the chance, Honduras have the players and flair to upset many high-profile opponents.

Argentina
All down to Messi

Group F

Argentina were runners-up in the 1930 FIFA World Cup, have won it twice and produced a harvest of the game's greatest players. Mario Kempes provided the winning goals in 1978 and Diego Maradona the inspiration in 1986. Now the weight of responsibility is carried by Lionel Messi. Barcelona's oft-crowned World Player of the Year has scored goals in abundance everywhere – except in the FIFA World Cup. Leading Argentina to victory in northern neighbour Brazil would be the ultimate seal on his status.

FACT FILE

Founded: 1893
National stadium: Monumental, Buenos Aires
Nickname: Albiceleste
Route to the finals: Winners of CONMEBOL group
FIFA World Ranking: 3
FIFA World Cup Finals appearances: 15
Winners: 1978, 1986
Ones to watch: Lionel Messi, Sergio Aguero, Angel Di Maria
Coach: Alex Sabella

Sergio Aguero scored key goals in Argentina's Beijing 2008 Olympic Games triumph.

Barcelona's Javier Mascherano can secure the heart of the defence or play a midfield anchor role.

Splat Stat
Argentina were top scorers in South American qualifying with 35 goals. Three players scored 24 of them: Leo Messi with 10, Gonzalo Higuain nine and Sergio Aguero five.

With the talent at their disposal no one will write off Argentina's chances of glory.

Bosnia-Herzegovina

New kids on the block

Group F

Bosnia-Herzegovina are making their FIFA World Cup finals debut only 22 years after the ethnically complex country split from the former Yugoslavia. But they have threatened to join the elite before. The Dragons lost only in qualifying play-offs for both the 2010 FIFA World Cup and Euro 2012. They reached Brazil after losing only one game in a group whose toughest rivals were Greece and Slovakia. The only man with FIFA World Cup 'previous' is coach Safet Susic who played in the finals for Yugoslavia in 1982 and 1990.

FACT FILE

Founded: 1992

National stadium: Bilino Polje, Zenica

Nickname: Dragons

Route to the finals: Winners of UEFA Group G

FIFA World Ranking: 19

FIFA World Cup Finals appearances: None

Winners: None

Ones to watch: Asmir Begovic, Edin Dzeko, Vedad Ibisevic

Coach: Safet Susic

Vedad Ibisevic (9) has played in Switzerland the US, France and Germany, but never in Bosnia.

Splat Stat

Four players – Edin Dzeko, Vedad Ibisevic, Asmir Begovic and Emir Spahic – played in all 10 of Bosnia-Herzegovina's qualifying matches. Dzeko (10) and Ibisevic (eight) scored 18 goals between them.

Edin Dzeko is Bosnia's all-time, 33-goal, top scorer.

After twice suffering playoff heartbreak, Bosnia-Herzegovina has at last qualified for a major finals.

Iran
Progress within reach

Group F

Reza Ghoochannejhad shot to fame in the closing stages of the FIFA World Cup qualifiers. Born in Iran but brought up in the Netherlands, he came to the attention of coach Carlos Queiroz through his goals for Sint-Truiden in Belgium. Reza made his Iran debut in autumn 2012 then hit five goals in four games against Lebanon, Qatar and South Korea to propel Team Melli to the finals in Brazil. Iran, long a power in Asian football, have yet to progress beyond the FIFA World Cup first round. Queiroz believes such a breakthrough is long overdue.

FACT FILE

Founded: 1920
National stadium: Azadi Stadium, Tehran
Nickname: Team Melli
Route to the finals: 4–0, 1–0 (5–0 on agg) v Maldives; winners of AFC third round, Group E; winners of fourth round, Group A
FIFA World Ranking: 33
FIFA World Cup Finals appearances: 3
Winners: None
Ones to watch: Javad Nekounam, Mohammad Nosrati, Ali Karimi
Coach: Carlos Queiroz

2006 FIFA World Cup veteran Ali Karimi is nicknamed the "Asian Maradona".

Splat Stat
Iran scored a memorable 2–1 victory over the United States at the 1998 FIFA World Cup in France, a match marked by its sporting spirit despite diplomatic tension between the nations.

Iran were joint leading scorers in the Asian qualifiers with 30 goals.

Javed Nekonam was a top contender for the 2013 Asian Player of the Year prize.

Nigeria
High flying Eagles

Group F

Nigeria approach the 2014 FIFA World Cup inspired by the greatest year in their national team history. In the spring of 2013, the Super Eagles won the Africa Cup of Nations for the first time in nearly two decades and, a few months later, their youngsters roared away with the FIFA Under-17 World Cup in Abu Dhabi. Nigeria have reached four of the last five FIFA World Cup finals and twice advanced into the second round. A crucial presence for the Super Eagles is Stephen Keshi, who was captain of the African champions in 1994 and coach of the team in 2013.

FACT FILE

Founded: 1945
National stadium: Abuja Stadium, Abuja
Nickname: Super Eagles
Route to the finals: Winners of CAF second round Group F then 2–1, 2–0 (4–1 agg) v Ethiopia
FIFA World Ranking: 37
FIFA World Cup Finals appearances: 4
Winners: None
Ones to watch: Vincent Enyeama, Victor Moses, John Obi Mikel
Coach: Stephen Keshi

Splat Stat
In 1994, after reaching the FIFA World Cup finals for the first time, Nigeria rose to fifth in the FIFA World Rankings. It remains the highest ever position achieved by an African nation.

Victor Moses switched to Nigeria after playing for England Under-21s.

John Obi Mikel anchors midfield for the three-times African champions.

Nigeria won 11 and lost only three of their 22 international matches in 2013.

Germany
Striking for glory

Group G

German football is as admired as that of Spain. The consistency of the national team, the production line of talent and the club brilliance of Bayern Munich and Borussia Dortmund has installed Joachim Low's team as possible first-ever European winners of the FIFA World Cup in the Americas. The Germans have both won the Cup and finished runners-up three times. But a fourth triumph depends on the strikers. Mesut Ozil was their leading scorer, from midfield, in the qualifying competition with eight goals.

FACT FILE

Founded: 1900
National stadium: Allianz Arena, Munich/ Olympiastadion, Berlin
Nickname: Die Nationalmannschaft
Route to the finals: Winners of UEFA Group C
FIFA World Ranking: 2
FIFA World Cup Finals appearances: 17
Winners: 1954, 1974, 1990 (all as West Germany)
Ones to watch: Mesut Ozil, Philipp Lahm, Thomas Muller
Coach: Joachim Low

Bastian Schweinsteiger is a rock at the heart of the German midfield.

Thomas Muller won the Golden Shoe at the 2010 FIFA World Cup with five goals and three assists.

Splat Stat
German legend Franz Beckenbauer is the only man to have won the FIFA World Cup as captain, in 1974, and as manager, in 1990. He was also local organising president in 2006.

Thrice winners and contenders every tournament – this is why the Germans are always a threat.

Portugal
Relying on Ronaldo

Group G

Portugal, ever since finishing third on their FIFA World Cup finals debut with Eusebio in 1966, have flattered to deceive on the biggest stage. Too often, exits have come as a result of self-inflicted wounds. Even this time Portugal needed a play-off victory over Sweden to reach the finals. Yet they will command widespread attention through the attacking genius of Cristiano Ronaldo, supported by Pepe and Fabio Coentrao in defence and Joao Moutinho in midfield. Portugal's fans crave something at least as good as their 2012 UEFA European Championship semi-final achievement.

FACT FILE

Founded: 1914
National stadium: Estadio de Honra, Lisbon
Nickname: Selecao das Quinas (Team of the Shields)
Route to the finals: Runners-up in UEFA Group F then 1–0, 3–2 (4–2 agg) v Sweden
FIFA World Ranking: 5
FIFA World Cup Finals appearances: 5
Winners: None
Ones to watch: Cristiano Ronaldo, Pepe, Joao Moutinho
Coach: Paulo Bento

Cristiano Ronaldo scored all four goals in Portugal's play-off victory.

Pepe was voted among the world's most outstanding defenders last year.

Splat Stat
Cristiano Ronaldo, in the play-off return against Sweden, scored his fifth hat-trick of the season to draw level with Pauleta as Portugal's all-time leading marksman on 47 goals.

Portugal needed the play-offs to qualify for a second FIFA World Cup in a row.

Ghana
Making up for lost time

Group G

Ghana were the first black African nation to star at international level but, for all their history and potential, did not reach the FIFA World Cup finals until 2006. They have also won the Africa Cup of Nations four times and FIFA world age-group events on three occasions. In the South Africa FIFA World Cup 2010, the Black Stars were the only one of six African nations to progress from the group stage and ended up just a shoot-out away from becoming the first African country to reach the semi-finals. Stars such as Asamoah Gyan and Kevin-Prince Boateng want to emulate that achievement.

FACT FILE

Founded: 1920
National stadium: Kumasi Sports Stadium, Ashanti
Nickname: Black Stars
Route to the finals: Winners of CAF second round Group D then 6–1, 1–2 (7–3 agg) v Egypt
FIFA World Ranking: 24
FIFA World Cup Finals appearances: 2
Winners: None
Ones to watch: Michael Essien, Asamoah Gyan, Kevin-Prince Boateng
Coach: Akwasi Appiah

Asamoah Gyan was Ghana's six-goal top marksman in the qualifiers for Brazil.

Kevin-Prince Boateng is a half-brother of Germany's Jerome Boateng.

Splat Stat
Ghana, at the Barcelona 1992 Games, became the first African football team to win an Olympic medal. They defeated Australia 1–0 in the third-place play-off to win the bronze medal.

At the 2010 FIFA World Cup Ghana became the third quarter-finalists from Africa.

United States
The American dream

Group G

The ambition to win a FIFA World Cup was sparked initially when the North American Soccer League was at its giddy heights in the 1970s. Some 40 years and 14 national coaches further on and Team USA have yet to progress beyond the quarter-finals. Pursuing that goal is coach Jurgen Klinsmann, returning to the finals in which he was a 1990 winner with West Germany. Equally determined to end his FIFA World Cup career on a high note will be Team USA's 32-year-old captain Landon Donovan, appearing in his fourth finals.

FACT FILE

Founded: 1913
National stadium: RFK Memorial, Washington DC
Nickname: Team USA
Route to the finals: Winners of CONCACAF third round Group A; winners of fourth round
FIFA World Ranking: 14
FIFA World Cup Finals appearances: 9
Winners: None
Ones to watch: Tim Howard, Landon Donovan, Clint Dempsey
Coach: Jurgen Klinsmann

A consistent goalscorer, Jozy Altidore has led the United States' attack in world finals at every age level.

Splat Stat
Former FIFA World Cup midfielder Cobi Jones ranks in the top 10 of the world's all-time international footballers after winning 164 caps, though he managed only 15 goals.

Clint Dempsey is Team USA's second-top goalscorer in history.

Team USA won 11 of 16 games and scored 26 goals in qualifying for the 2014 FIFA World Cup.

Belgium
The young generation

Group H

After 12 bleak years Belgium have not only returned to the FIFA World Cup finals but returned as one of the most intriguing of teams. The Red Devils reached the 1986 FIFA World Cup semi-finals and their fans have waited ever since for a comparable team. The new version, fashioned by coach Marc Wilmots, is built around a new generation, strong in each department – from Vincent Kompany in central defence to Eden Hazard and Romelu Lukaku in attack. Coach Wilmots is Belgium's five-goal all-time leading scorer in the finals.

FACT FILE

Founded: 1895
National stadium: Roi Baudouin, formerly Heysel, Brussels
Nickname: Red Devils
Route to the finals: Winners of UEFA Group A
FIFA World Ranking: 11
FIFA World Cup Finals appearances: 11
Winners: None
Ones to watch: Vincent Kompany, Eden Hazard, Romelu Lukaku
Coach: Marc Wilmots

Eden Hazard has sharpened his big-game experience with Premier League Chelsea.

Splat Stat
Belgium's 18 goals during qualifying were shared among 10 players. Kevin de Bruyne top-scored with four. Romelu Lukaku's two goals were the ones which beat Croatia in a decisive game.

Marouane Fellaini offers the support of goals from midfield.

Belgium have climbed more than 50 places in the FIFA World Rankings since 2009.

Algeria
Roadmap for progress

Group H

Algeria's FIFA World Cup finals debut in 1982 ended in a narrow and unfortunate first round exit and the Desert Foxes have yet to go beyond the group stage after two further tries. Their prospects in Brazil depend on exporting their magnificent home form: in four qualifying matches in Blida they conceded only one goal. And it was in front of those same fans that a single goal from veteran captain Madjid Bougherra edged them past Burkina Faso on away goals in the play-off second leg, after a 3–2 defeat in Ouagadougou. Algeria were Africa's last qualifiers for the finals in Brazil.

FACT FILE

Founded: 1962
National stadium: Mustapha Tchaker, Blida
Nickname: Desert Foxes
Route to the finals: Winners of CAF second round Group H then 2–3, 1–0 (away goals, 3–3 agg) v Burkina Faso
FIFA World Ranking: 26
FIFA World Cup Finals appearances: 3
Winners: None
Ones to watch: Madjid Bougherra, Islam Slimani, Saphir Taider
Coach: Vahid Halilhodzic

Splat Stat
Portugal-based Islam Slimani, from Sporting Lisbon, top-scored for Algeria in the qualifiers with five goals, five years after having been called up for the first time to the national squad.

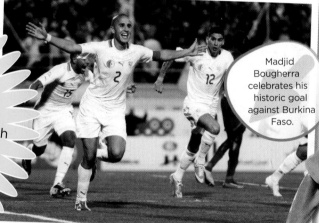

Madjid Bougherra celebrates his historic goal against Burkina Faso.

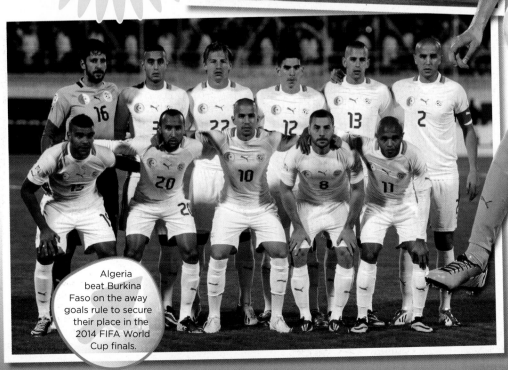

Algeria beat Burkina Faso on the away goals rule to secure their place in the 2014 FIFA World Cup finals.

Islam Slimani scored nine goals in 17 games for Algeria in only 18 months.

Russia
Bear necessities

Group H

Fabio Capello took England to the 2010 FIFA World Cup finals but their second-round exit almost cost him the job. The 2018 hosts, by contrast, would be pleased to progress that far. One of Europe's giants, Russia repeatedly punch below their weight. The Russian bear lost to Slovenia in the 2010 play-offs and crashed in the first round at Euro 2012. Finally, they edged top spot in Group F by one point from Cristiano Ronaldo's Portugal thanks to the talents of keeper Igor Akinfeyev and sharp-shooting Alexander Kerzhakov.

FACT FILE

Founded: 1912 (Russia), 1946 (Soviet Union), 1991 (Russia)

National stadium: Luzhniki, Moscow

Nickname: Sbornaya

Route to the finals: Winners of UEFA Group F

FIFA World Ranking: 22

FIFA World Cup Finals appearances: 9

Winners: None

Ones to watch: Igor Akinfeyev, Sergey Ignashevich, Alexander Kerzhakov

Coach: Fabio Capello

Igor Akinfeyev was a league regular at 17 and a senior international at 18.

Alexander Kerzhakov is a finals veteran, after playing in the 2002 FIFA World Cup in Japan/Korea.

Splat Stat
Lev Yashin, who played 94 times for the old Soviet Union between 1954 and 1967, was the only goalkeeper ever awarded the Ballon d'Or as European Footballer of the Year.

The hosts in 2018, Russia will want to set a precedent for success in Brazil.

Korea Republic
Olympic inspiration

Group H

Coach Hong Myung-Bo represents continuity in Korean football. He captained the co-hosts at the 2002 FIFA World Cup then became youth and Olympic coach. Thus he is relying on a nucleus of the young players who finished third at London 2012. These include centre-back Hong Jeong-Ho plus captain Koo Ja-Cheol. The latter, from Germany's Mainz 05, was the top scorer at the 2011 Asian Cup. He also demonstrated his eye for goal with the strike which clinched victory over Japan in the Olympic bronze medal play-off.

FACT FILE

Founded: 1928
National stadium: Seoul World Cup Stadium
Nickname: Taeguk Warriors
Route to the finals: Runners-up in AFC fourth round Group A
FIFA World Ranking: 54
FIFA World Cup Finals appearances: 8
Winners: None
Ones to watch: Lee Jung-Soo, Lee Chung-Yong, Park Chu-Young
Coach: Hong Myung-Bo

Park Chu-Young won a bronze medal at the London 2012 Olympic Games.

Splat Stat
Korea, managed by Dutchman Guus Hiddink, became the only Asian nation ever to reach the last four of the FIFA World Cup when they co-hosted the finals with Japan in 2002.

Lee Chung-Yong was hailed as one of the rising stars on view at the 2010 FIFA World Cup.

Korea Republic were semi-finalists in 2002, but a repeat would be an even greater shock in 2014.

45

Players to Watch:

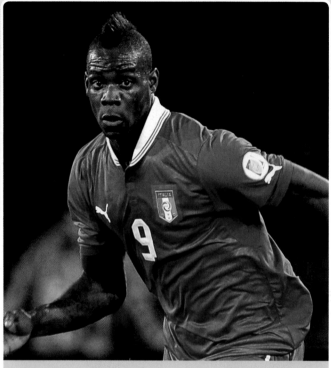

MARIO BALOTELLI

Country:	Italy
Club:	AC Milan
Position:	Forward
Born:	12 August 1990
Appearances:	29
Goals:	12

Skills and strengths: Powerful forward who uses his aggressive strength and powerful shot to strike fear into the hearts of defenders at home and abroad. Always a danger at free kicks around goal.

Goals and glory: 'Super Mario' exploded onto the scene at Euro 2012 where he scored twice in Italy's semi-final win over Germany. Followed up with a winner against Mexico in the FIFA Confederations Cup.

Claim to fame: The son of Ghanaian immigrants, he has sparked fireworks on and off the pitch in a club career at Internazionale, Manchester City and Milan.

LIONEL MESSI

Country:	Argentina
Club:	FC Barcelona (Spain)
Position:	Forward
Born:	24 June 1987
Appearances:	83
Goals:	37

Skills and strengths: Moves as if the ball is tied to his boots, ideally cutting in from the right and either swapping deft passes with his team-mates or shimmying through defences on his own.

Goals and glory: Messi, by 25, was hailed as the youngest player to score 200 Spanish league goals after already having become Barcelona's all-time top scorer in competitive football.

Claim to fame: Won his first title at the U-20 FIFA World Cup in 2005 followed by Olympic gold in 2008 plus four FIFA world player awards, two world club crowns and three Champions Leagues.

Forwards

NEYMAR

Country:	Brazil
Club:	FC Barcelona (Spain)
Position:	Forward
Born:	5 February 1992
Appearances:	46
Goals:	27

Skills and strengths: His speed, mesmeric control and shooting power not only turned Santos, Pele's old club, into South American champions but earned him a FIFA Goal of the Year award.

Goals and glory: As an 18-year-old Neymar scored 42 goals in 60 games in 2010, and was twice South American player of the year before being sold to FC Barcelona for £49 million in 2013.

Claim to fame: Led Santos to a first world club final in 50 years and scored in every match in Brazil's FIFA Confederations Cup 2013 triumph including the second goal in the final win over Spain.

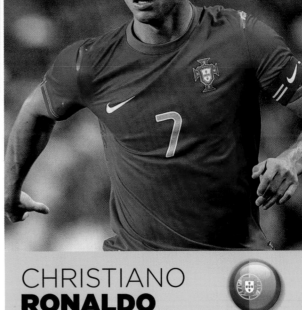

CHRISTIANO RONALDO

Country:	Portugal
Club:	Real Madrid (Spain)
Position:	Forward
Born:	5 February 1985
Appearances:	109
Goals:	47

Skills and strengths: Originally a teenage right winger who honed his talent to become the most excitingly dramatic all-round attacker in the game.

Goals and glory: Outstanding Ronaldo scored all four goals, including an away leg hat-trick, in Portugal's two-leg victory over Zlatan Ibrahimovic's Sweden in the 2014 FIFA World Cup play-offs.

Claim to fame: Ronaldo's hunger for goals since a then record £80m move to Real Madrid in 2009 has seen him outstrip the feats of legends such as Di Stefano and Puskas. He was named FIFA World Player of the Year – Men for 2013.

Players to Watch:

 WAYNE
ROONEY

Country:	England
Club:	Manchester United
Position:	Forward
Born:	24 October 1985
Appearances:	88
Goals:	38

Skills and strengths: At his best Rooney is a rampaging, irresistible force anywhere in the attacking third of the pitch; always aggressive, always focused on forging the most direct route to goal.

Goals and glory: Rooney cost United £25.6 million at 18, has won all major national and international club prizes and scored more than 200 club goals, United's fourth-highest of all time.

Claim to fame: When Rooney made his senior international debut in 2003 he was then the youngest player to represent England. He remains his country's youngest-ever goalscorer at 17.

THOMAS
MULLER

Country:	Germany
Club:	Bayern Munich
Position:	Forward
Born:	13 September 1989
Appearances:	47
Goals:	16

Skills and strengths: The latest Muller to threaten FIFA World Cup defences does so with pace, preferably off the right wing, matched with the rare skill to 'ghost' unnoticed into space in front of goal.

Goals and glory: Muller's best season thus far was 2012–13 when he hit 23 goals in all competitions helping Bayern land the Champions League and German league, cup and supercup.

Claim to fame: Ended his first full season by starring at the 2010 FIFA World Cup where Germany finished third and he was top marksman with five goals and three assists in six appearances.

Forwards

LUIS SUAREZ

Country:	Uruguay
Club:	Liverpool (England)
Position:	Forward
Born:	24 January 1987
Appearances:	76
Goals:	39

Skills and strengths: Suarez boasts the tightest control and sharpest acceleration all supported by the most unquenchable self-belief that he is destined to score a goal in each and every attack.

Goals and glory: Topped a century of goals in four years in all competitions for Ajax before moving to Liverpool and, at 27, is already Uruguay's all-time record marksman with 39 goals.

Claim to fame: Took a key role for Uruguay at the last FIFA World Cup but missed the semi-final defeat by Netherlands after being sent off for a goal-line handball against Ghana in the quarters.

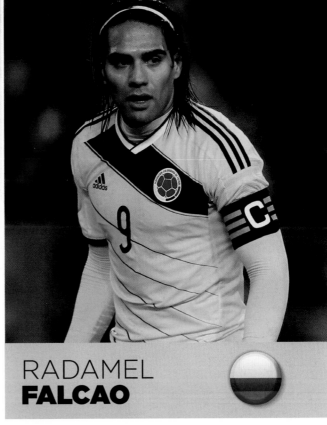

RADAMEL FALCAO

Country:	Colombia
Club:	Monaco (France)
Position:	Forward
Born:	10 February 1986
Appearances:	51
Goals:	20

Skills and strengths: Falcao not only possesses surprising pace and delicacy of touch for a powerful man but is the most unselfish of strikers, prepared to run all day long in the service of his team.

Goals and glory: 'El Tigre' racked up more than 100 goals in his first three seasons in Europe including a hat-trick against Chelsea as Atletico Madrid won the 2012 UEFA Supercup.

Claim to fame: Falcao scored a record 17 goals in European games in 2010–11 when Porto won the domestic treble unbeaten and topped it all off with Europa League success.

Players to Watch:

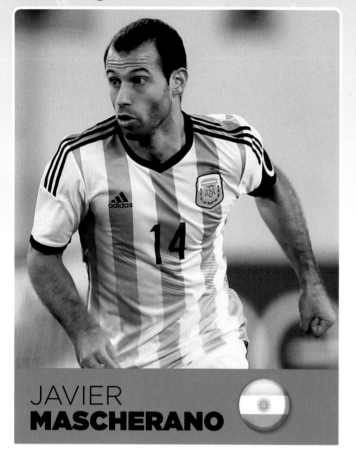

JAVIER MASCHERANO

Country:	Argentina
Club:	FC Barcelona (Spain)
Position:	Midfielder
Born:	8 June 1984
Appearances:	95
Goals:	2

Skills and strengths: Mascherano's ability to play as both a holding midfielder and as a central defender means that his judgment as a team 'anchor' is unmatched across the world game.

Goals and glory: Mascherano has only ever scored two goals for Argentina, against Paraguay and Peru in the 2007 Copa America, but has won league titles in Argentina, Brazil and Spain.

Claim to fame: When Argentina won the Olympic Games title in Beijing in 2008 Mascherano became the first footballer to have won two successive football gold medals since 1928.

PAULINHO

Country:	Brazil
Club:	Tottenham Hotspur (England)
Position:	Midfielder
Born:	25 July 1988
Appearances:	24
Goals:	5

Skills and strengths: Paulinho earned new fans at the FIFA Confederations Cup 2013 by mixing his attacking eye with a readiness for defensive support work and a goal-scoring threat in the air at set pieces.

Goals and glory: Scored what proved the winner for Brazil over Uruguay in the semi-final of the FIFA Confederations Cup and was later voted third in the tournament top player poll.

Claim to fame: Played in Lithuania and Poland before settling back in Brazil at Corinthians with whom he won the Copa Libertadores and FIFA World Club Cup before joining Tottenham.

Midfielders

STEVEN GERRARD

Country:	England
Club:	Liverpool
Position:	Midfielder
Born:	30 May 1980
Appearances:	108
Goals:	21

Skills and strengths: The younger Gerrard specialised in rescuing matches single-handed, while the older player applies his knowhow in a controlled manner across the full breadth of a match.

Goals and glory: Gerrard is the only player to have scored in the finals of the FA Cup, the League Cup, the UEFA Cup and, most memorably, the UEFA Champions League against Milan in 2005.

Claim to fame: Captain of Liverpool since 2003, 'Stevie G' captained England at Euro 2012 and was once described by Zinedine Zidane as the best all-round footballer in the world.

MESUT OZIL

Country:	Germany
Club:	Arsenal (England)
Position:	Midfielder
Born:	15 October 1988
Appearances:	52
Goals:	17

Skills and strengths: Epitomises the ideal modern footballer, working for the team, directing play in the centre of the pitch and providing both piercing assists and crucial goals of his own.

Goals and glory: In 2013 Ozil was assists leader in major European and domestic competitions after having been one of the top providers at the 2010 FIFA World Cup and Euro 2012.

Claim to fame: Ozil's transfer from Real Madrid for £42.5m in 2013 made him at once both Arsenal's most costly footballer and also the most expensive German player of all time.

Players to Watch:

ANDREA PIRLO

Country:	Italy
Club:	Juventus
Position:	Midfielder
Born:	19 May 1979
Appearances:	107
Goals:	13

Skills and strengths: Even in his mid-30s Pirlo's economy of movement allows him to combine a magnetism of the ball with inch-perfect passing – and a teasing penalty-kick style.

Goals and glory: Played for Italy at all youth levels before his senior debut in 2002. He topped the assists chart in Italy's 2006 FIFA World Cup triumph. He's a winner of 13 major honours at club level.

Claim to fame: Hailed by master coach Carlo Ancelotti as "the greatest player I ever worked with," and labelled The Architect by his Italy team-mates for creating so many of their goals.

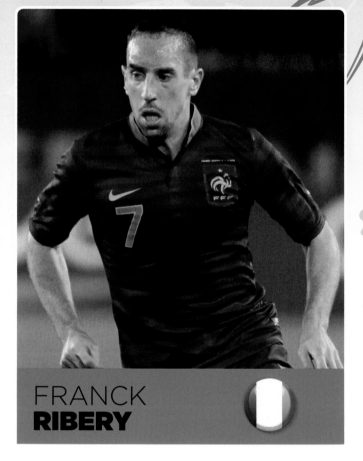

FRANCK RIBERY

Country:	France
Club:	Bayern Munich (Germany)
Position:	Midfielder
Born:	7 April 1983
Appearances:	80
Goals:	16

Skills and strengths: Ribery enjoys tormenting defences from the space he finds on the wings though successive coaches have also sought to harness his vision in a playmaking role.

Goals and glory: In his international career Ribery has contributed more assists (20) than goals (16) for Les Bleus. His first goal was against Spain during his FIFA World Cup 'explosion' in 2006.

Claim to fame: Ribery landed the UEFA best player accolade in 2013 after winning, with Bayern Munich, the hat-trick of German league and cup plus Champions League.

Midfielders

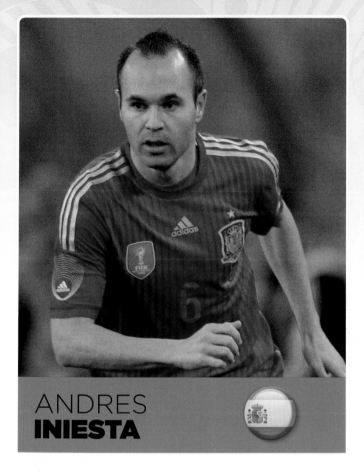

ANDRES INIESTA

Country:	Spain
Club:	FC Barcelona
Position:	Midfielder
Born:	11 May 1984
Appearances:	94
Goals:	11

Skills and strengths: The brilliance of Iniesta is that, even though opponents are well aware of his skill and one-touch genius, he manages repeatedly to find space enough to apply a killer touch.

Goals and glory: Though more creator than scorer, Iniesta wrote his name into football history with Spain's last-minute winner in the 2010 FIFA World Cup Final against Netherlands.

Claim to fame: Iniesta was a central member of Spain's 'titles hat-trick' team from 2008 to 2012 as well as the Barcelona side who won a unique six trophies in one calendar year in 2009.

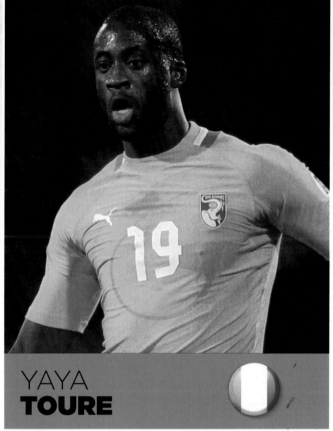

YAYA TOURE

Country:	Ivory Coast
Club:	Manchester City (England)
Position:	Midfielder
Born:	13 May 1983
Appearances:	82
Goals:	16

Skills and strengths: Yaya Toure possesses power and skill and a venomous shot but also outstanding tactical vision to adjust his role to the varying demands of any match situation.

Goals and glory: A Champions League winner with Barcelona in 2009 as centre back then scored winning goals from Manchester City's midfield in the 2011 FA Cup semi-final and final.

Claim to fame: Voted African Footballer of the Year three times and added the BBC's African player poll prize in 2013 after being among the leading nominees five times in succession.

Players to Watch:

PHILIPP LAHM

Country:	Germany
Club:	Bayern Munich
Position:	Defender
Born:	11 November 1983
Appearances:	104
Goals:	5

Skills and strengths: Lahm made his name as a full back but proved so stylish that, like Paul Breitner before him at Germany and Bayern, he can move forward to great effect when required.

Goals and glory: A perpetual danger at free kicks and distance, Lahm hit Germany's first goal in the 4–2 defeat of Costa Rica in the hosts' opening match at the 2006 FIFA World Cup Finals.

Claim to fame: Consistency underlined by status in the 'squad of the tournament' at the 2006 and 2010 FIFA World Cups, Euro 2008 and 2012 as well as four times in UEFA's Team of the Year.

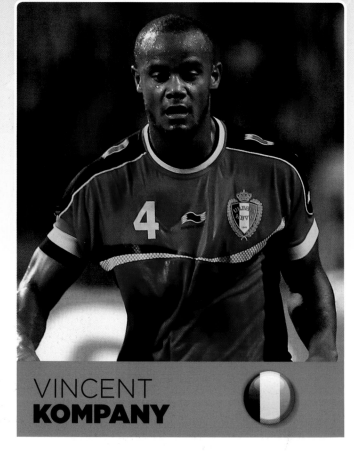

VINCENT KOMPANY

Country:	Belgium
Club:	Manchester City (England)
Position:	Defender
Born:	10 April 1986
Appearances:	56
Goals:	4

Skills and strengths: Kompany began as a wing back and defensive midfielder before settling into his established role at centre back where his organisational skills are best deployed.

Goals and glory: The Anderlecht discovery became one of Belgium's youngest ever internationals when he made his senior national team debut at 17 in February 2004 against France.

Claim to fame: Kompany took over the captaincy of Manchester City in 2011–12, the season the club carried off the English Premier League crown, their first league title in 44 years.

Defenders

THIAGO SILVA

Country:	Brazil
Club:	Paris Saint-Germain (France)
Position:	Defender
Born:	22 September 1984
Appearances:	44
Goals:	2

Skills and strengths: Thiago Silva has proved himself a commanding presence for club and country both on the pitch and off it, a title-winning rock in a storm in central defence for Brazil and PSG.

Goals and glory: Won league titles in Italy and France with Milan and Paris Saint-Germain then captained Brazil to FIFA Confederations Cup success one year out from the FIFA World Cup.

Claim to fame: FIFA World Cup victory in July would more than adequately make amends for Thiago Silva's bitter Olympic disappointment of 'only' bronze in 2008 and silver in 2012.

SERGIO RAMOS

Country:	Spain
Club:	Real Madrid
Position:	Defender
Born:	30 March 1986
Appearances:	115
Goals:	9

Skills and strengths: Sergio Ramos, with the experience of more than a century of caps, has learned the secret of sharp timing in the tackle to temper the ferocious defending of his early days.

Goals and glory: In 2013, Ramos became, at 26, the youngest European player to reach 100 caps and celebrated by opening the scoring in a 1–1 draw with Finland in the FIFA World Cup qualifiers.

Claim to fame: Another member of the exclusive Spanish band to have starred in the triumphant treble of 2010 FIFA World Cup plus the European Championships of 2008 and 2012.

Players to Watch:

GIANLUIGI BUFFON

Country: Italy
Club: Juventus
Position: Goalkeeper
Born: 28 January 1978
Appearances: 138

Skills and strengths: Buffon, with more caps to his name than even the great Dino Zoff, has proved an equally inspiring captain of Italy with his superb reflexes and cool demeanour.

Goals and glory: One of Buffon's many crucial penalty saves was one from England's Ashley Cole in Italy's shootout success on the way to the Euro 2012 final in Poland and Ukraine.

Claim to fame: Buffon cost Juventus a world record €51m. He is the Azzurri's record international and won the Yashin Award after Italy's FIFA World Cup victory in 2006.

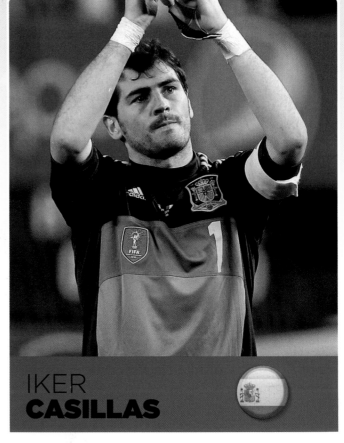

IKER CASILLAS

Country: Spain
Club: Real Madrid
Position: Goalkeeper
Born: 20 May 1981
Appearances: 152

Skills and strengths: As both a captain and a goalkeeper Casillas, with his speed of thought, secure handling and 'sweeper-keeper' style, has led a revolution in the goalkeeping role.

Goals and glory: A one-club man, having played his entire 24-year career with Real Madrid, Casillas has represented Spain at every age level and won 19 trophies for club and country.

Claim to fame: Casillas holds a unique record as the only player – never mind goalkeeper – to have captained the winning team in the FIFA World Cup and two European Championships.

Goalkeepers

MANUEL NEUER

Country: Germany
Club: Bayern Munich
Position: Goalkeeper
Born: 27 March 1986
Appearances: 44

Skills and strengths: Neuer sets a high standard for all the current generation of goalkeepers with his defensive communication, secure footwork, plus intelligent distribution of the ball.

Goals and glory: Won the Champions League at the end of only his second season with Bayern to put him up alongside legendary old club heroes such as Sepp Maier and Oliver Kahn.

Claim to fame: Had the cool-headed presence of mind to play on, against England at the 2010 FIFA World Cup, after the match ball spun back into play after Frank Lampard's 'phantom goal.'

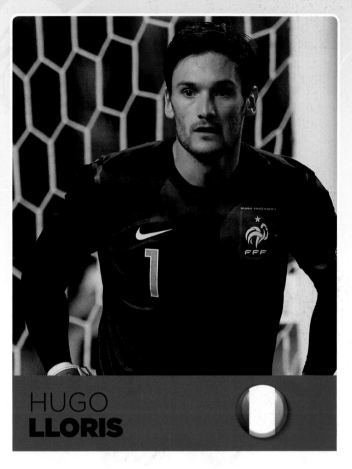

HUGO LLORIS

Country: France
Club: Tottenham Hotspur (England)
Position: Goalkeeper
Born: 26 December 1986
Appearances: 54

Skills and strengths: Lloris's skills extend beyond all the basic box-bossing technical essentials to include decisiveness, speed off his line and courage in the face of an onrushing striker.

Goals and glory: Nicknamed 'Saint Lloris' by the media after his superb displays in the qualifying play-off against the Irish Republic which saw France reach the finals of the 2010 FIFA World Cup.

Claim to fame: One of the few players to emerge with his reputation enhanced despite Les Bleus' first-round exit at the 2010 FIFA World Cup – after which he was appointed national captain.

FIFA World Cup™ Picture Quiz

They say every picture tells a story. Can you work out what's what in the following football foursomes?

CAPTAIN FANTASTIC

Who are these mysterious skippers, and which countries do they play for?

A

B

C

D

THE HEAT IS ON ...

Who are these coaches going through the emotions on the touchline, and which countries will they be attempting to guide to glory at the 2014 FIFA World Cup?

A

B

C

D

SO GLAD WE'VE MADE IT

Which teams are overjoyed to have qualified for the finals of the 2014 FIFA World Cup, and who did they knock out in the process?

A

B

C

D

WE ARE THE CHAMPIONS

Can you name the year and host nation of the FIFA World Cup shown in these celebratory scenes as well as the exultant winners of the Trophy in each case?

FIFA World Cup™ Trivia Quiz

So you think you're pretty clued up about the history of the FIFA World Cup. Test your knowledge with this mega football trivia quiz. You'll find the answers on page 59. But no sneaky peaking – or you'll be shown the red card!

HISTORY

1 Who was the first man to have won the FIFA World Cup both as a player and a manager?
2 What was the name of the stadium in Uruguayan capital Montevideo that staged the first FIFA World Cup final, in 1930?
3 Which FIFA World Cup was the first to feature penalty shoot-outs, four years after they were introduced for the finals?
4 Who was the first man to play at five different FIFA World Cups?
5 What was the name of the dog that found the FIFA World Cup trophy after it had been stolen in England ahead of the 1966 tournament?
6 Which Brazilian city staged the famous upset at the 1950 FIFA World Cup when England lost 1–0 to the United States?
7 Which is the only country to compete in every FIFA World Cup finals?
8 Which country will host the FIFA World Cup in 2018?
9 Which man has coached a team at the most different FIFA World Cups (six)?
10 What FIFA World Cup milestone was set by France's Lucien Laurent?

WINNERS

1 Who scored Argentina's winner in their 3–2 victory over West Germany in the 1986 FIFA World Cup final?
2 Who scored Spain's extra-time winner against the Netherlands in the 2010 FIFA World Cup final?
3 How many years old was Pele when he won the FIFA World Cup for the first time in 1958, with further glory
to follow in 1962 and 1970?
4 Who won the Golden Ball, for best player, at the 2010 FIFA World Cup?
5 How many Argentina players were voted into FIFA's All-Star Team of the tournament in 1986, when crowned champions
6 Who were the first winners of the current FIFA World Cup design after it replaced the previous Jules Rimet trophy?
7 Who scored Uruguay's winning goal against Brazil to claim the 1950 FIFA World Cup, in Rio's Maracana stadium?
8 How many matches at FIFA World Cup finals – including the victorious 1990 final – has Germany's Lothar Matthaus played, more than any other footballer?
9 After a rule-change meaning only FIFA World Cup host countries automatically took part, who were the first reigning FIFA World Cup champions who had to progress through qualifiers for the next finals?
10 Who is the only person to have twice won the FIFA World Cup as manager?

FIFA World Cup™ Picture Quiz (see pages 59-59) – Answers
Captain Fantastic: A Cristiano Ronaldo (Portugal). **B** Didier Drogba (Ivory Coast). **C** Hugo Lloris (France). **D** Antonio Valencia (Ecuador).
The Heat is On ...: A Vicente Del Bosque (Spain). **B** Fabio Capello (Russia). **C** Luiz Felipe Scolari (Brazil). **D** Joachim Löw (Germany).
So Glad We've Made It: A Nigeria (Ethiopia). **B** Portugal (Sweden). **C** Mexico (New Zealand). **D** France (Ukraine).
We Are the Champions: A 2006 FIFA World Cup Germany (Italy). **B** 2010 FIFA World Cup South Africa (Spain). **C** 2002 FIFA World Cup Korea/Japan (Brazil). **D** 1998 FIFA World Cup France (France).

NATIONS

1 Which country was the original choice to host the 1986 FIFA World Cup, only to withdraw and be replaced by Mexico in 1983?
2 Which was the only team not to lose a game at the 2010 FIFA World Cup?
3 When did England compete in their first FIFA World Cup finals?
4 Which was the first host country not to reach the second round?
5 Which is the only country to reach the final of three different FIFA World Cups without winning any?
6 Which was the only FIFA World Cup to feature all four of the British home nations England, Northern Ireland, Scotland and Wales?
7 Which country has qualified for the FIFA World Cup most often (eight times) without reaching the second round once?
8 Which country holds the record for most goals scored in one FIFA World Cup (27) even though they failed to win the tournament?
9 What precedent did Switzerland set at the 2006 FIFA World Cup?
10 England have taken part in the most FIFA World Cup penalty shoot-outs without a win – how many?

GOALS

1 Who is the only man to score a hat-trick in a FIFA World Cup final?
2 Who is the only player to score for both teams in one match?
3 Who was the first player to score a FIFA World Cup hat-trick?
4 How many goals did Golden Boot-winner Just Fontaine, of France, score at the 1958 FIFA World Cup a record for a single tournament?
5 How many goals has Brazilian forward Ronaldo scored in FIFA World Cup final tournaments, an all-time record?
6 Which Argentina striker is the only man to score a hat-trick at two different FIFA World Cups?
7 Which Russia striker is the only man to score five goals in one FIFA World Cup match?
8 Who is the youngest player to score a FIFA World Cup hat-trick?
9 Marcos Coll's goal for Colombia against the USSR in 1962 remains unique in FIFA World Cup history – why?
10 Who is both the FIFA World Cup's oldest player and oldest goalscorer?

MISCELLANEOUS

1 Who was the English referee who awarded the first penalty in a FIFA World Cup final, for the Netherlands against West Germany in the first minute of their 1974 showdown?
2 WWho was the first player sent off at a FIFA World Cup?
3 Zinedine Zidane is one of only two players to be sent off at two different FIFA World Cups – who is the other?
4 Who was the first player sent off in a FIFA World Cup final?
5 Which country has scored most own goals overall in the FIFA World Cup?
6 Who missed the final spot-kick as Italy lost the 1994 FIFA World Cup final to Brazil in a penalty shoot-out?
7 Which year was the only FIFA World Cup not to feature a hat-trick?
8 Who was the first player to win the Yashin Award for best goalkeeper, introduced at the 1994 FIFA World Cup?
9 Who holds the record for youngest player at a FIFA World Cup, being aged 17 years and 41 days for his first appearance at the 1982 tournament?
10 Which FIFA World Cup holds the record for highest average attendance per match (68,991)?

2014 FIFA World Cup Brazil™ – Match Schedule

GROUP A

12 June, 17:00	Brazil	3	1 Croatia	Sao Paulo
13 June, 13:00	Mexico	1	0 Cameroon	Natal
17 June, 16:00	Brazil	0	0 Mexico	Fortaleza
18 June, 18:00	Cameroon	0	4 Croatia	Manaus
23 June, 17:00	Cameroon	1	4 Brazil	Brasilia
23 June, 17:00	Croatia	1	3 Mexico	Recife

Team	P	W	D	L	GD	Pts
1 Brazil		1		0	+5	
3 Croatia		1	0	1		
2 Mexico		1			+3	
4 Cameroon			0	1	-8	

GROUP B

13 June, 16:00	Spain	1	5 Netherlands	Salvador
13 June, 18:00	Chile		3 Australia	Cuiaba
18 June, 16:00	Spain	0	2 Chile	Rio de Janeiro
18 June, 13:00	Australia	2	3 Netherlands	Porto Alegre
23 June, 13:00	Australia	0	3 Spain	Curitiba
23 June, 13:00	Netherlands	2	0 Chile	Sao Paulo

Team	P	W	D	L	GD	Pts
3 Spain			0		+3	
1 Netherlands			0	0	+7	
2 Chile			0		+2	
4 Australia		0	0		-6	

GROUP C

14 June, 13:00	Colombia	3	0 Greece	Belo Horizonte
14 June, 22:00	Ivory Coast	2	1 Japan	Recife
19 June, 13:00	Colombia	2	1 Ivory Coast	Brasilia
19 June, 19:00	Japan	0	0 Greece	Natal
24 June, 16:00	Japan	1	4 Colombia	Cuiaba
24 June, 17:00	Greece	2	1 Ivory Coast	Fortaleza

Team	P	W	D	L	GD	Pts
1 Colombia			0	0	+7	
3 Ivory Coast			0		-1	
4 Japan		0			-4	
2 Greece			1		-2	

GROUP D

14 June, 16:00	Uruguay	1	3 Costa Rica	Fortaleza
14 June, 18:00	England	1	2 Italy	Manaus
19 June, 16:00	Uruguay	2	1 England	Sao Paulo
20 June, 13:00	Italy	0	1 Costa Rica	Recife
24 June, 13:00	Italy	0	1 Uruguay	Natal
24 June, 13:00	Costa Rica	0	0 England	Belo Horizonte

Team	P	W	D	L	GD	Pts
3 Italy			0		-1	
4 England			0		-2	
1 Costa Rica			1	0	+3	
2 Uruguay			0		0	

GROUP E

15 June, 13:00	Switzerland	2	1 Ecuador	Brasilia
15 June, 16:00	France	3	0 Honduras	Porto Alegre
20 June, 16:00	Switzerland	2	5 France	Salvador
20 June, 19:00	Honduras	1	2 Ecuador	Curitiba
25 June, 16:00	Honduras	0	3 Switzerland	Manaus
25 June, 17:00	Ecuador	0	0 France	Rio de Janeiro

Team	P	W	D	L	GD	Pts
1 France					+6	
4 Honduras					-9	
2 Swiss					+1	
3 Ecuador					0	

GROUP F

15 June, 19:00	Argentina	2	1 Bosnia	Rio de Janeiro
16 June, 16:00	Iran	0	0 Nigeria	Curitiba
21 June, 13:00	Argentina	1	0 Iran	Belo Horizonte
21 June, 18:00	Nigeria	1	0 Bosnia	Cuiaba
25 June, 13:00	Nigeria	2	3 Argentina	Porto Alegre
25 June, 13:00	Bosnia	3	1 Iran	Salvador

Team	P	W	D	L	GD	Pts
1 Argentina			0	0	+3	
3 Bosnia					0	
4 Iran			0		-3	
2 Nigeria					0	